Pigs

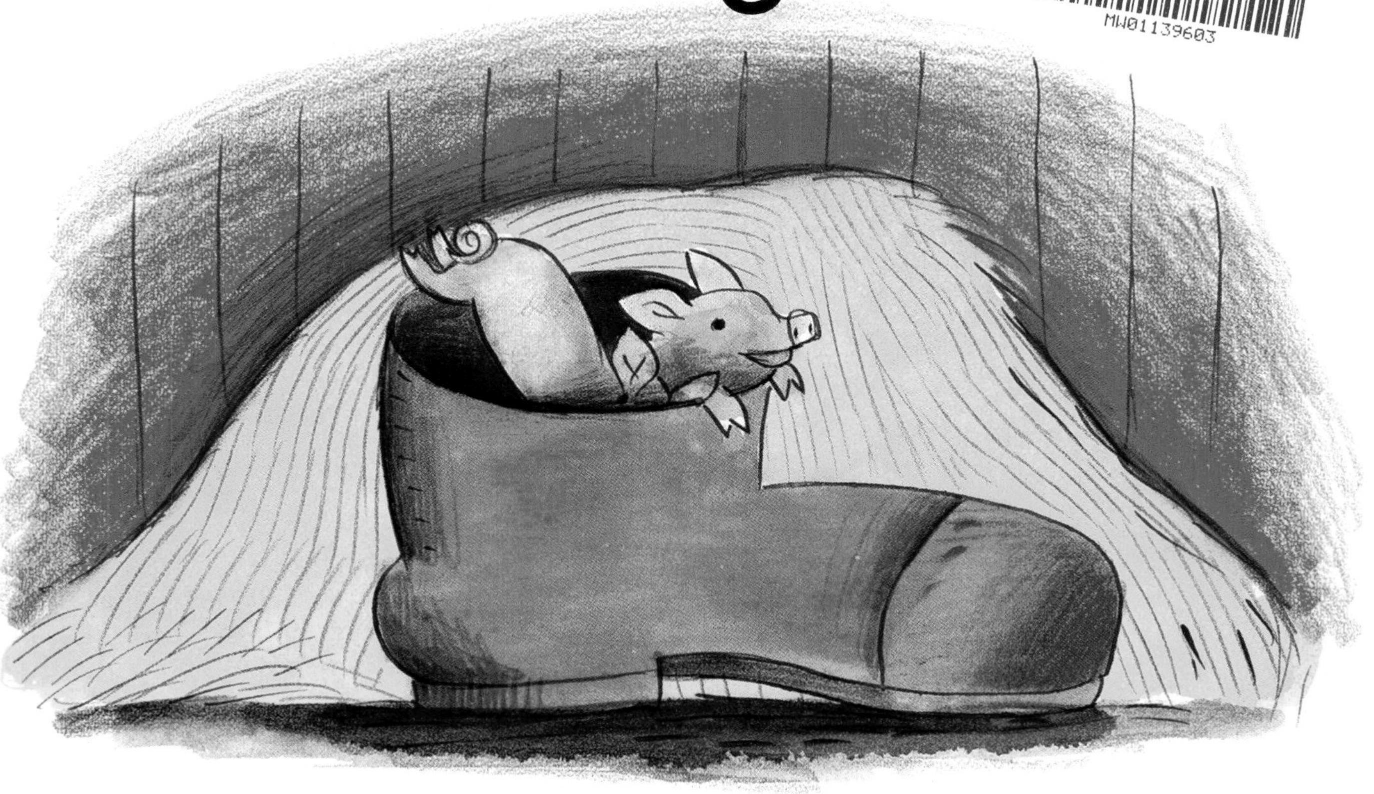

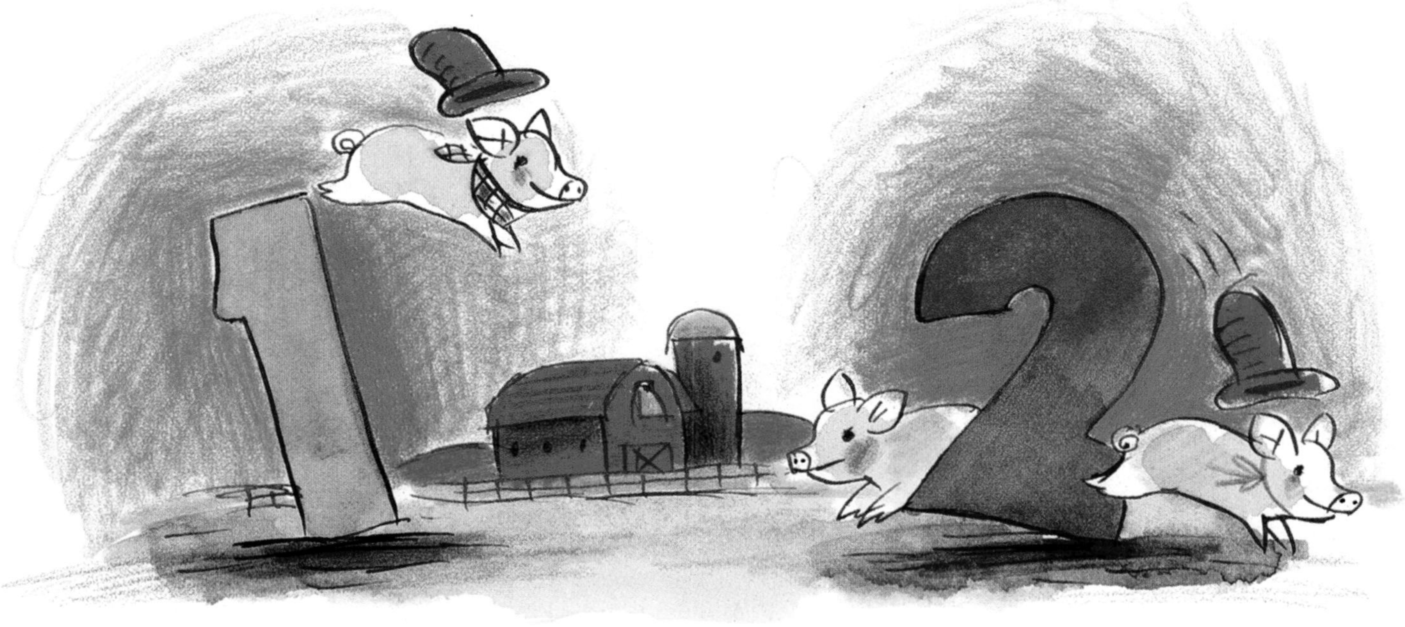

One, two

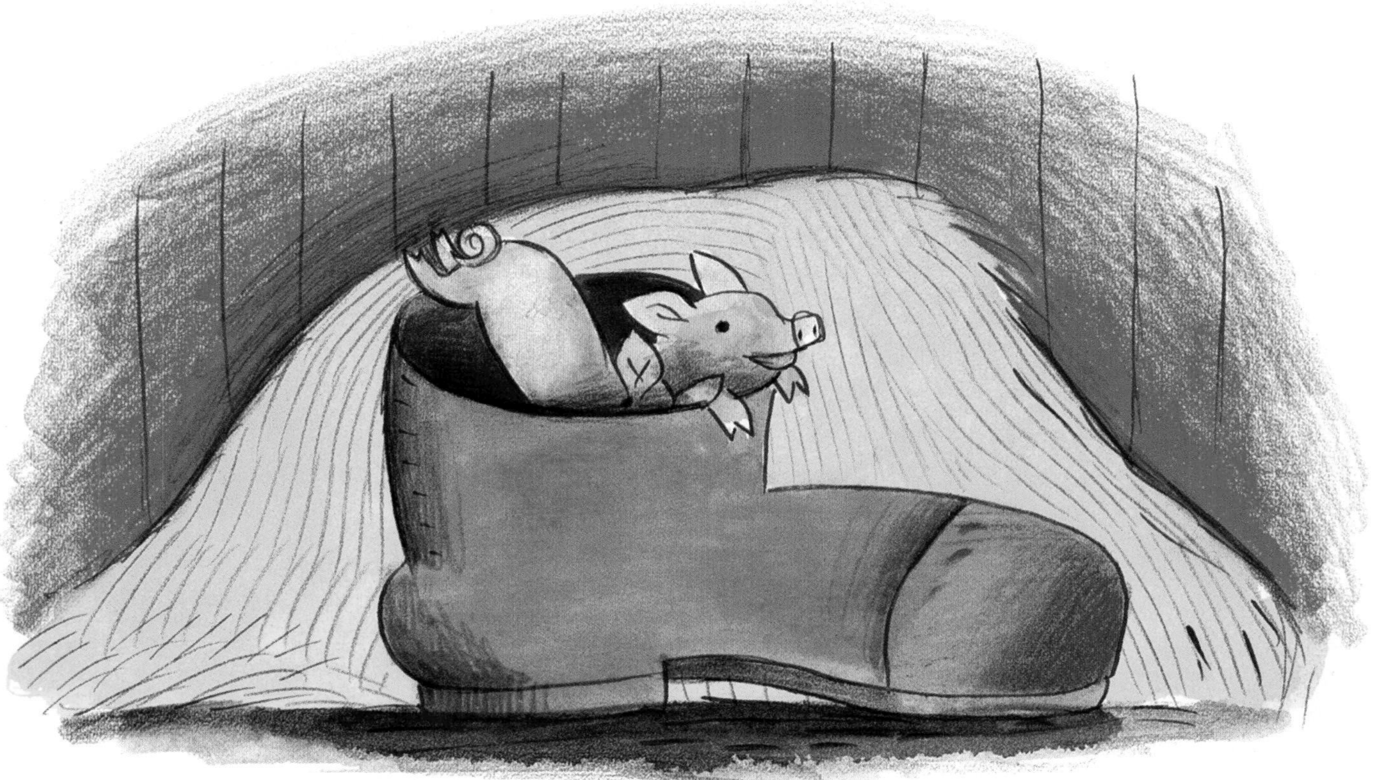

Pigs in a shoe.

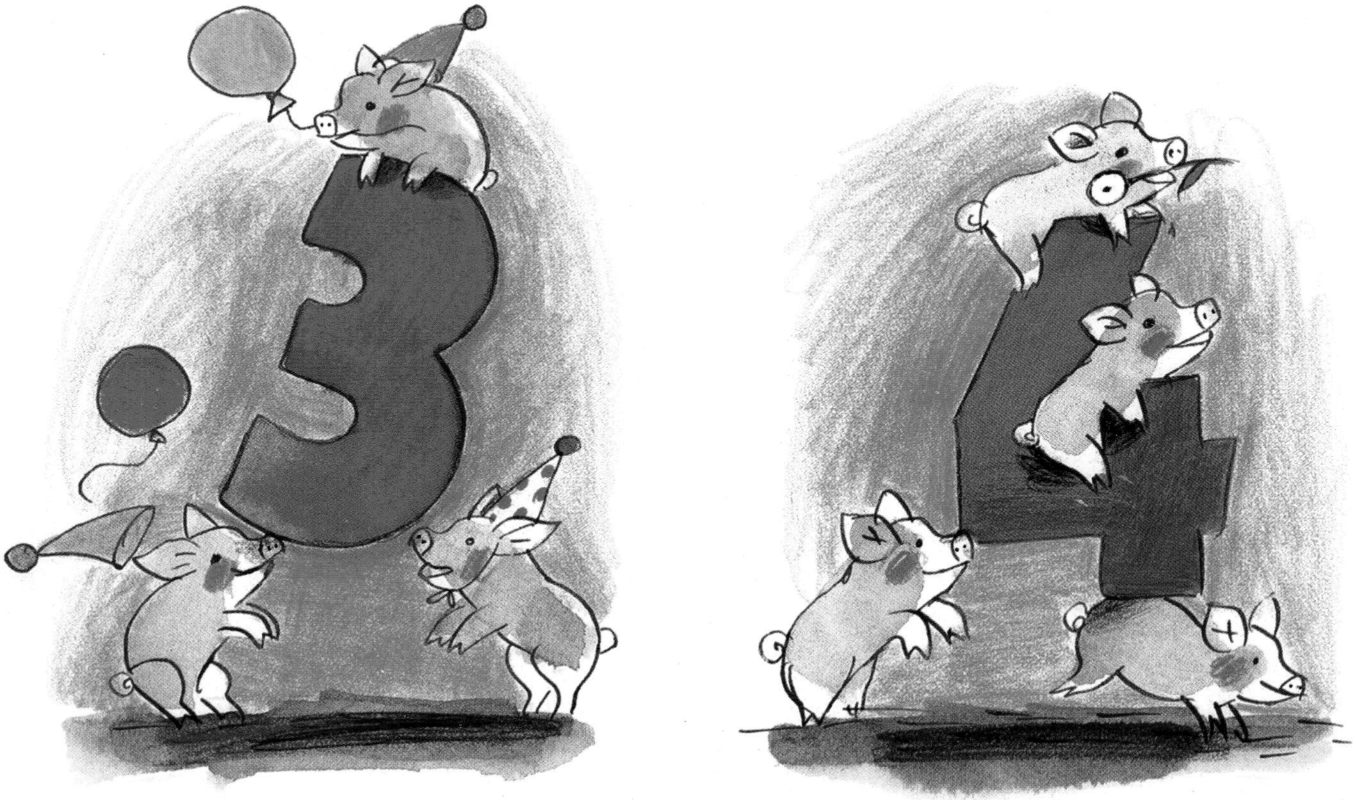

Three, four

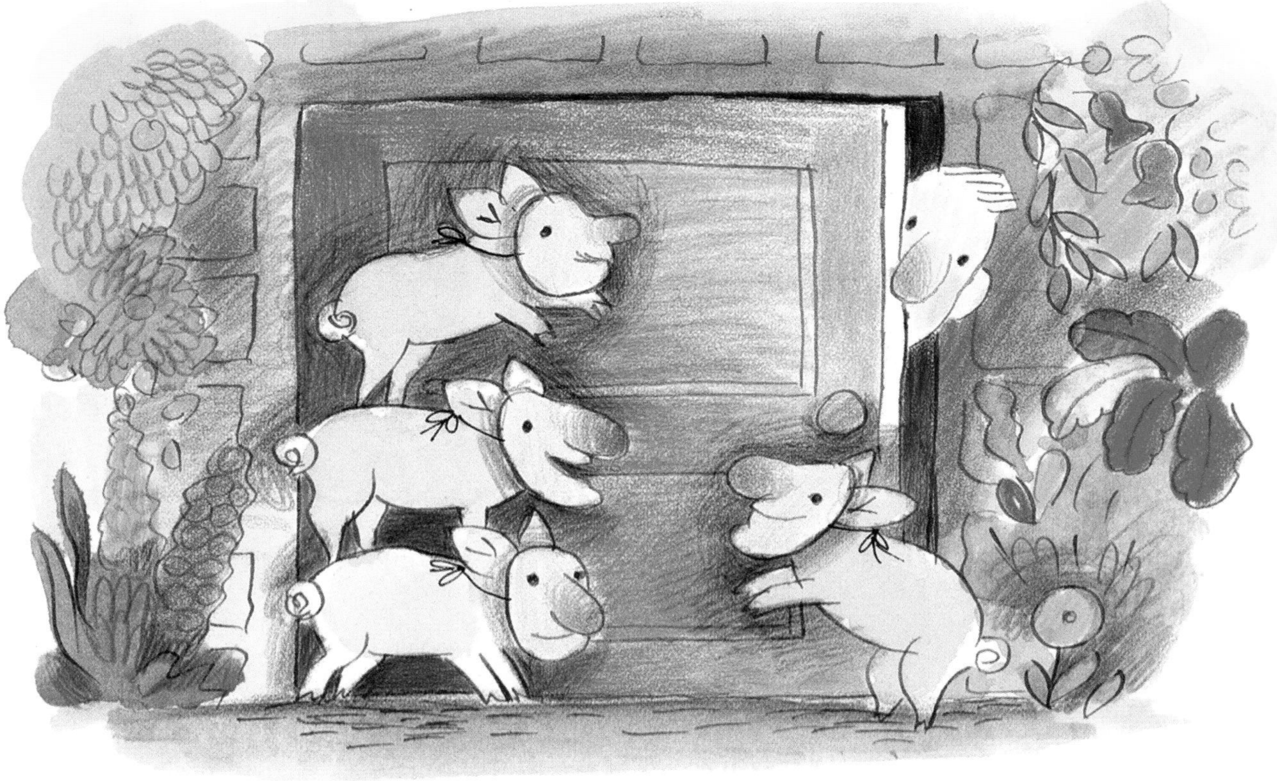

Pigs at the door.

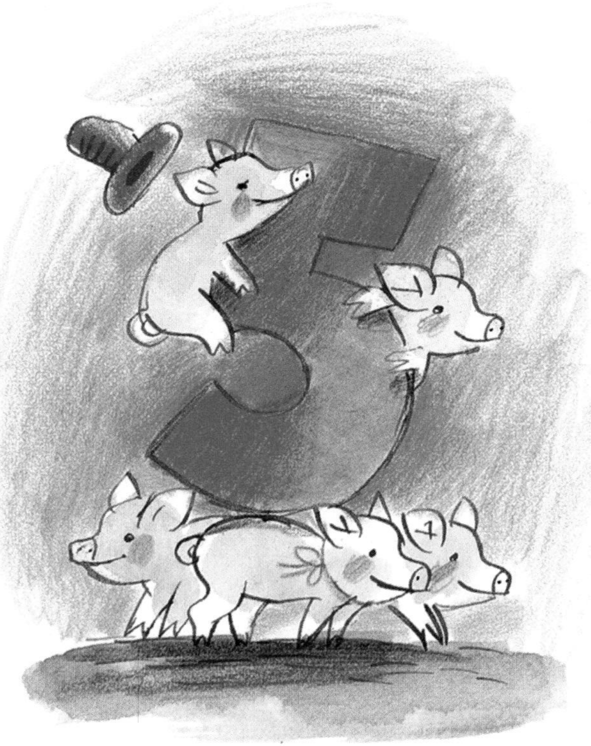

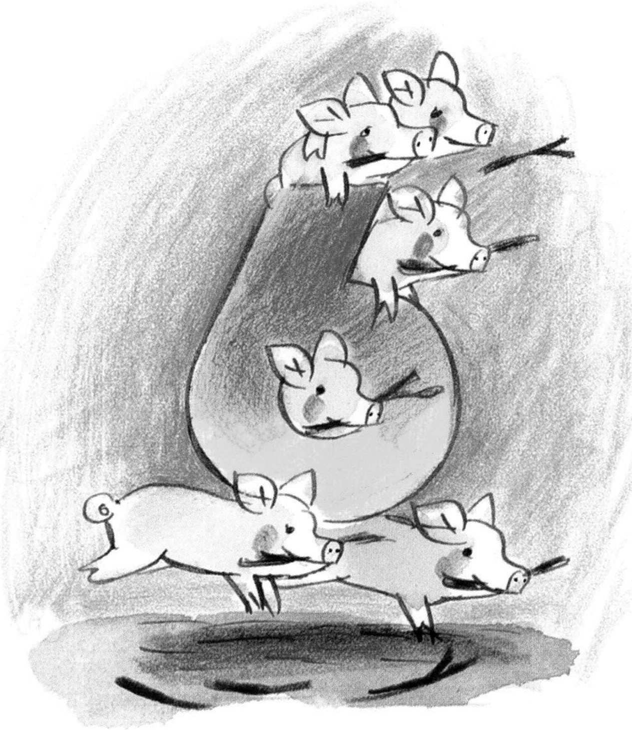

Five, six
Pigs with sticks.

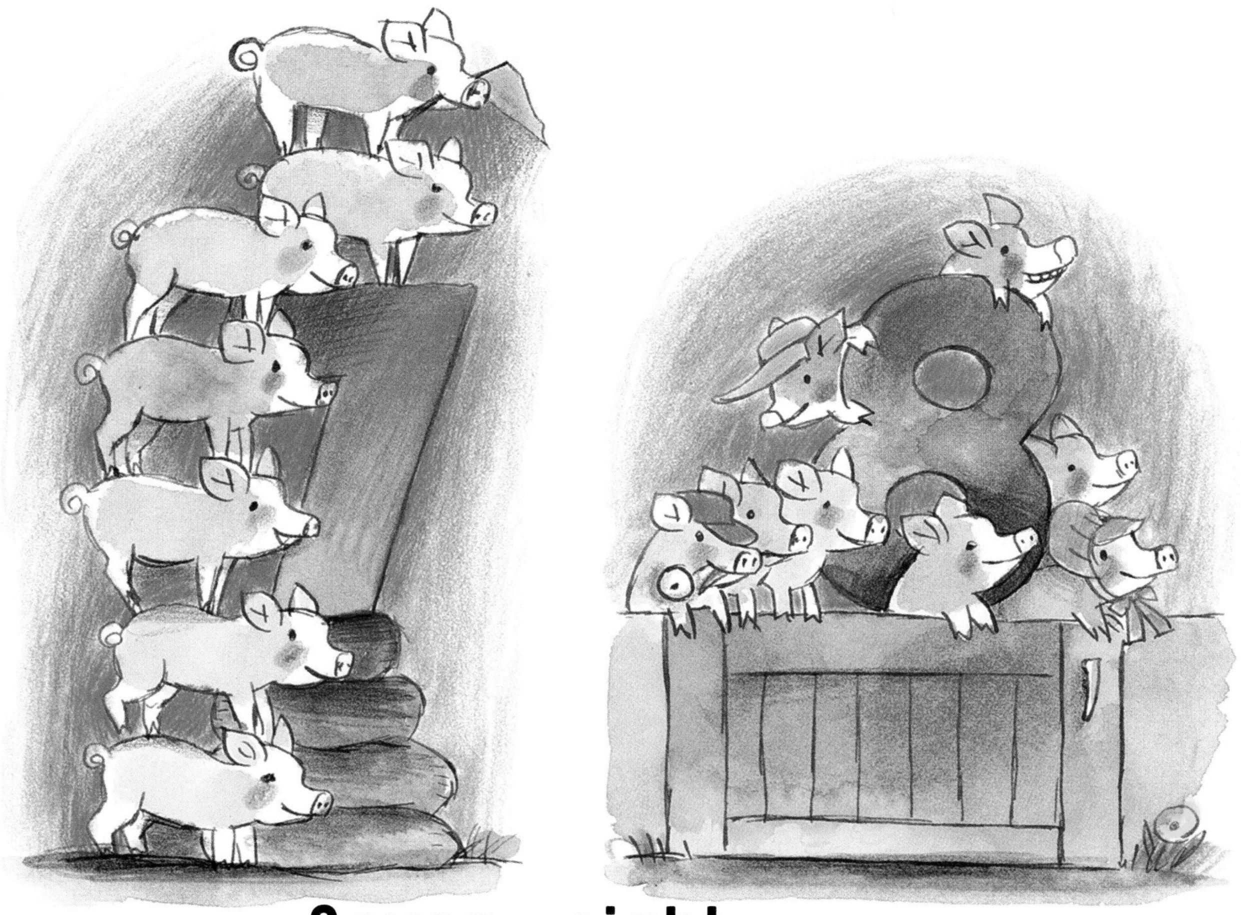

Seven, eight
Pigs on the gate.

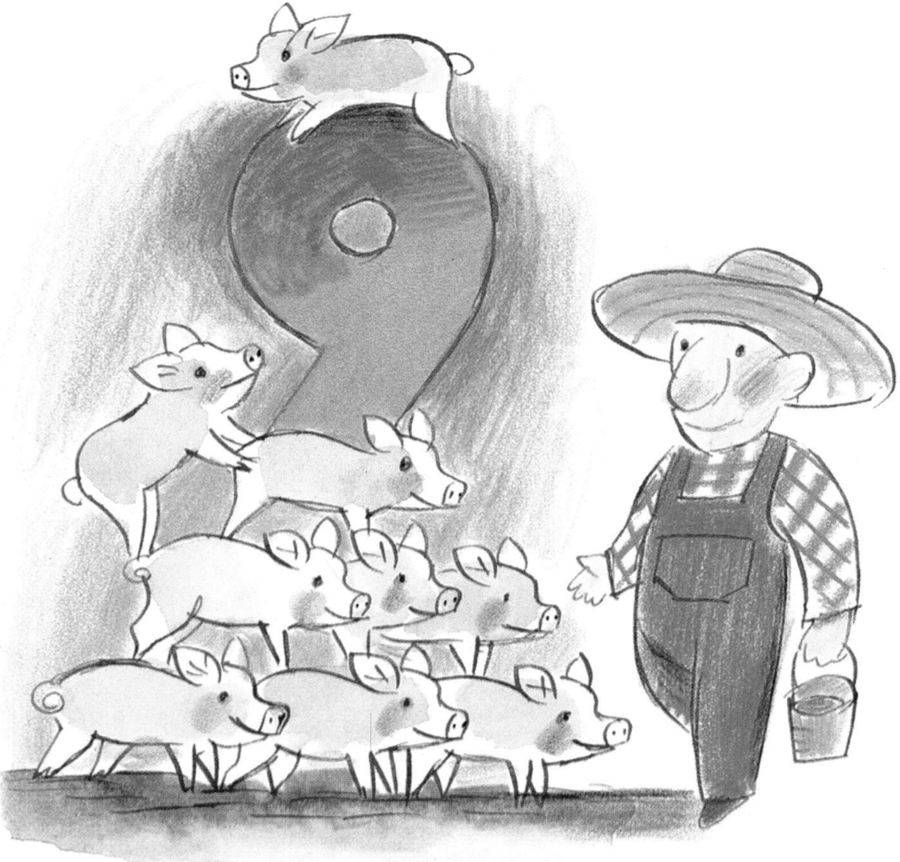

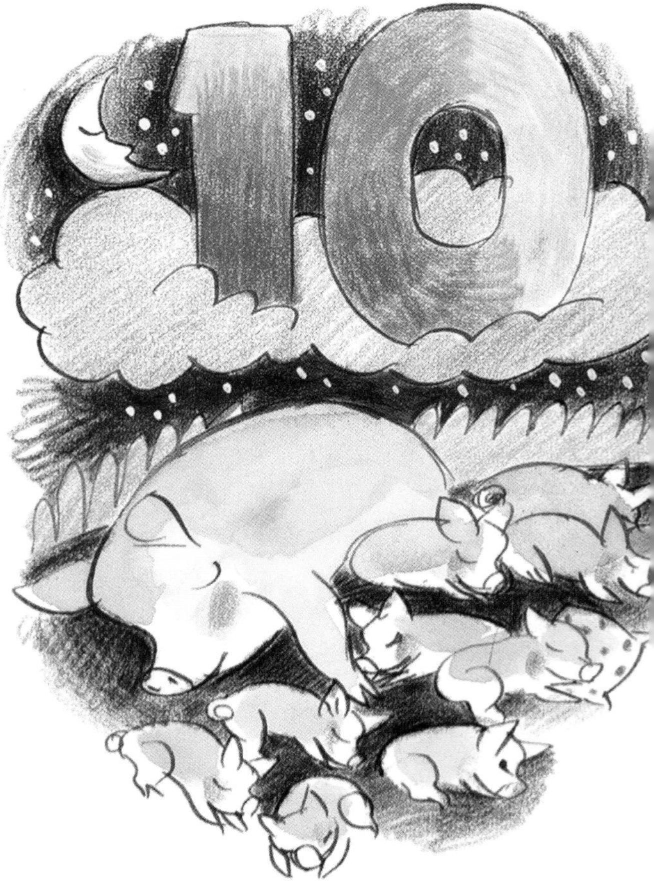

Nine, ten
Pigs in a pen!